ISBN (Paperback) 978-1-955364-36-2
ISBN (Ebook) 978-1-955364-37-9
Vets Publish
www.vetspublish.com

A is for Algorithm

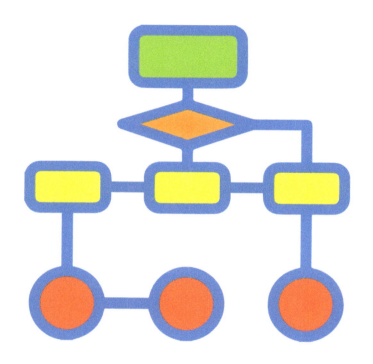

A step by step plan

B is for Bug

An error in computer land

C is for Coding

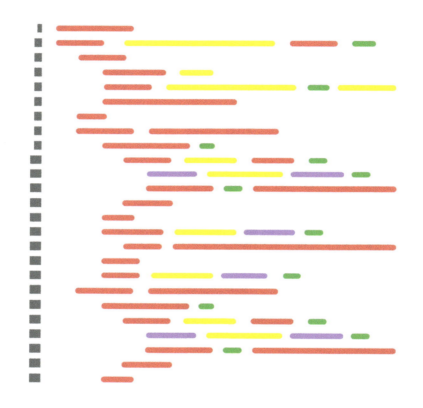

Written lines
of instruction

D is for Debugging

Fixing any disruption

E is for Error

A mistake
we can find

F is for function

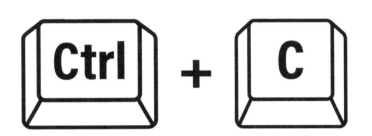 Ctrl + C

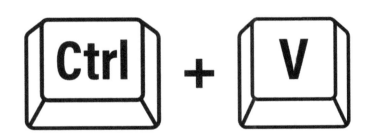 Ctrl + V

A reusable design

G is for graphics

Adding colors
and shapes

H is for HTML

Building webpages
with grace

I is for Input

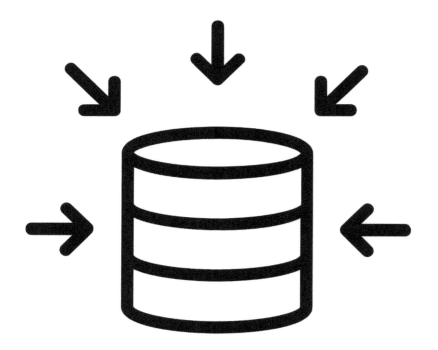

Data we receive

J is for JavaScript

```
1   define([
2       'can',
3       'models/account',
4       'controls/dashboard/dashboard',
5       'controls/misc/titlebar',
6       'toastr',
7       'moment',
8       'utils/helpers'
9   ], function(can, Account, Dashboard, Titlebar,
10      return can.Control.extend({
11          defaults: new can.Map({
12              success: null,
13              error: null,
14              username: null,
15              password: null
16          })
17      },{
        init: function() {
```

Making
websites acheive

K is for Keyboard

Where we
type commands

L is for Loop

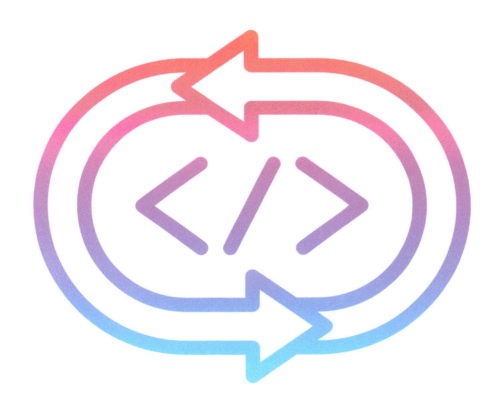

Repeating code
again and again

M is for Mouse

Navigating the screen

N is for Null

Where nothing is seen

O is for Output

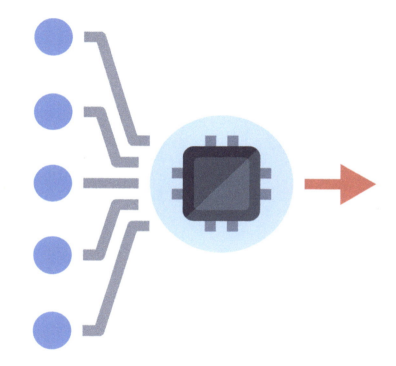

The results we can see

P is for programing

A skill for you and me

Q is for Query

Asking questions
in code

R is for Recursion

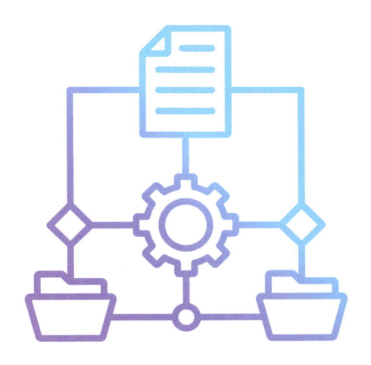

A function
that is reloaded

S is for Syntax

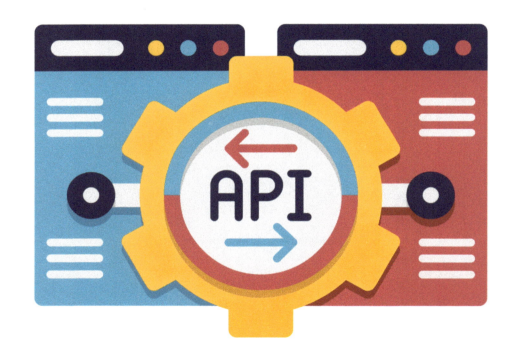

Rules to Obey

T is for Terminal

Where commands
we say

U is for URL

A website's address

V is for Variable

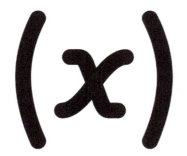

Values we possess

W is for While Loop

Looping with care

X is XML

Data we share

Y is for YAML

A format for configuration

Z is for Zip

Compressing files
with dedication